EALING

THEN & NOW

IN COLOUR

DR JONATHAN OATES & PAUL HOWARD LANG

The History Press

This book is dedicated to both of our Carolines.

First published in 2012

The History Press
The Mill, Brimscombe Port
Stroud, Gloucestershire, GL5 2QG
www.thehistorypress.co.uk

ISBN 978 0 7524 6374 2

Typesetting and origination by The History Press
Printed in India.
Manufacturing managed by Jellyfish Print Solutions Ltd

CONTENTS

ACKNOWLEDGEMENTS

The authors wish to thank Tasmin Lang for her help with the photography in this book; Paul Champion for his anecdote about Ho Chi Minh; Paul Fitzmaurice for his comments; and David Blackwell for sharing his knowledge about Hanwell.

INTRODUCTION

This book takes forty-five pairs of views of Ealing, one from the early twentieth century alongside the same view a century later, to compare the changes and developments that have taken place during the intervening years. However, before we examine these views, old and new, we need to consider the bigger picture.

Ealing in 1911 was a newly formed borough in Middlesex, whose boundaries roughly corresponded to that of the post-1863 parish. By 2011, Ealing was a London Borough which had absorbed the neighbouring parishes of Acton, Southall, Greenford, Perivale, Northolt and Hanwell, and thus whose boundaries are wider yet. In 1911, it had a population of 61,222 (having had 33,031 in 1901). In 2001, the population numbered 300,948. Although Ealing's population is almost certainly not wholly British-born, even in 1911, the contrast was still great. In 2001, 19,142 people were born in Europe and 93,169 from the rest of the world, mostly Asia. Nearly 50,000 residents described themselves as Indian, with 13,507 black people and 31,769 from other Asian countries. In 1901, almost all of Ealing's inhabitants were born within the British Isles, though only a minority were born in Ealing itself.

Ealing, then as now, enjoyed a number of forms of transport. There was the Great Western Railway (now First Great Western), with stations at Ealing Broadway and West Ealing. Then there was the District Underground line, with stations at Ealing Broadway, Ealing Common, South Ealing and Northfields. After the First World War, the Central line extended as far west as Ealing. In 1901, the London United Tramways system arrived, which ran along the Uxbridge Road, from Shepherd's Bush to Uxbridge (by 1904). This had been a very controversial scheme and there had been much opposition prior to its

4

inception. There were also buses serving the borough, but no trams since 1936 (despite recent attempts to reintroduce them). Motorcars were few and far between in 1911, with only a single garage in Ealing. By 2011 there are few households within the borough without a car.

Ealing's schools were certainly diverse. There were no council-run schools in Ealing until 1903, as the borough had relied on Church schools financed by voluntary subscriptions. By the end of 1911 there were six primary schools throughout the borough and a further eleven Church schools. There were also a number of private schools, most of which were single sex, unlike the council schools. The same could be said of the situation now, with some surviving from a century ago, such as St Benedict's and Heidelburg (renamed Harvington during the First World War). The Technical Institute provided for higher education in 1911; its successor is the University of West London.

At the beginning of the twentieth century there were few industries in Ealing, but the one which was to make Ealing internationally known still exists to this day; the Ealing Film Studios. One industry which has declined, though, is domestic service. A hundred years ago, it was the most common form of female employment, and most employees 'lived in'. Today, the employment of part-time cleaners is more common.

Ealing's principal shopping streets 100 years ago were the Mall, Ealing Broadway, the High Street and West Ealing Broadway. One of the major department stores in Ealing was owned by Eldred Sayers, who was deputy mayor in 1910-1911. Established in 1837, it claimed to have 'the finest selection of Drapery west of Oxford Street'.

Ealing in 1911 was undergoing much change. The same can be said of Ealing now, as the Dickens' Yard development behind the Town Hall will further develop the site in regard to retail and additional housing.

From the early twentieth century, Ealing prided itself on being 'the Queen of the Suburbs' and was described in the following manner: 'Ealing Broadway is now a thriving thoroughfare in the centre of an equally thriving town, which stretches from Acton to Hanwell, from Brentford to Perivale . . . the man who earns his living in Cheapside no longer lives over his business. He finds some healthy, economical, well managed suburb, and goes out from the smoky city each evening to his healthy, invigorating country atmosphere. For such may the atmosphere of Ealing be called, since a quarter of an hour's walk from the centre stretches the open countryside, here meadows and hedges, there woods and hills and streams'.

Estate agents today still use the same points of reference as they did a hundred years ago: 'It has all the ingredients necessary – including fine Victorian houses, interesting local shops and acres of green space – to lure young families away from more expensive and fashionable parts of west London. It also has transport links that are hard to beat'.

Dr Jonathan Oates, 2012

ST ALBANS' CHURCH

THIS RED BASILICA on Acton Green has certainly seen many changes since it was built
in 1887-1888 by local architect and, later, councillor Edward Monson. The building to the
right of the church was the parish hall. It merged with the parish of All Saints in 1982. This
is ironic because All Saints existed for nearly two decades before St Albans. Then, St Albans

was but a mission church of All Saints. The new church developed slowly, and was consecrated on 16 June 1888 by the Bishop of London. In 1900, the chancel and apse were added, followed by the vestries in 1914. The main building cost £3,500 and could seat 700 worshippers. Between 1888 and 1988 there were ten vicars, with the Revd Stanley Arthur Spackman being the longest serving, from 1929 to 1953. The church will not be here much longer as major plans for the site's redevelopment are being planned.

CONGREGATIONAL
CHURCH, ACTON

THE CONTRAST BETWEEN these
two pictures is startling. Acton
Congregational Church, on the
corner of Churchfield Road West
and Spencer Road, was built in 1871
by J. Tarring & Son. The building on
the right is the church hall. The first
pastor was the Revd William Adeney,
and there was much activity at this
time. The church had a Band of Hope
and a Sons of Temperance Movement
in order to encourage sobriety and
thrift among the working classes.
There was also a Pleasant Sunday
Afternoon club for men, as well as
an active Sunday school. However,
the Congregationalists merged with
the Presbyterians to form the United
Reform Church in 1972. From 1978
they used the former Methodist church
on Acton Hill and disposed of this one.
It was demolished and flats built on the
site in 1978-1979, to accommodate
twenty-nine elderly people.

ST MARY'S CHURCH

EALING'S PARISH CHURCH, St Mary's, has altered little between these two views. Had we compared views of the church from the early nineteenth to the early twentieth century, the changes would have been significant, as the Georgian box church was transformed into what we see today by S.S. Teulon in the 1860s. Opinion on this style of architecture – Teulon's personal style of High Victorian Gothic – is sharply divided. There was major internal refurbishment in recent times and in 2004 the Civic Society gave the church an award for this.

CHRIST CHURCH

IN OUTWARD APPEARANCE, this Gilbert Scott church has not changed much in the intervening century, nor indeed since it was consecrated in 1852 (although the pinnacles of the church were destroyed during the Second World War and not replaced). Rather, it is the surroundings which have altered. The trees of the earlier era are no longer with us, nor are the tramlines or overhead tram wires. The people, too, are wearing different apparel, with both sexes wearing hats and the ladies in skirts in the 1920s, whereas the women of 2011 wear trousers and only one wears headgear. The other difference, unbeknown to any casual viewer, is that the name of the church is different. It is now Christ the Saviour, following a parochial merger with St Saviour's Church in the 1950s. Its first two vicars both attracted publicity, though for different reasons. The Revd William Lambert, the elderly first incumbent, achieved notoriety by frequenting séances locally and for an alleged affair with a young female parishioner. He was replaced by the Revd Joseph Hilliard, who founded social clubs and a church school, which still exists today. A painting of him hangs in the Town Hall's Council Chamber.

ST PETER'S CHURCH, EALING

ST PETER'S CHURCH, designed in 1893 by John D. Sedding and Henry Wilson and thought by architectural historians to be the finest church in Ealing, has changed little externally and this is reflected in these two photographs. Sedding actually died before his ideas evolved much, so it was his assistant, Wilson, who did most of the work and created a church based on the Arts and Crafts ideas then prevalent. However, there have been numerous internal changes in the last century. John Dorey was the builder for this church, as well as for St Albans. A pulpit was constructed in 1910, a lady chapel at the rear in 1913, and

various ornamentation throughout the period. The Bishop of London, Frederick Temple, consecrated this church as he did St Albans, too. It is notable for its great west window, pictured here, which stands out in comparison to the mostly plain windows of this church.

ST MELLITUS CHURCH, HANWELL

THIS CARD SHOWS a remarkably deserted road with the impressive-looking St Mellitus Church standing on one side. It was designed by Sir Arthur Blomfield in 1910 and was Hanwell's third Anglican church and the first to have a separate parish carved out for it. In 1914, apart from two Sunday services, there was a monthly men's service and women's service. The church has a very unusual and eye-catching bell-cote of brick and stone with three bells inset. The church is in the Gothic revival style in brown and buff brick, with doors and windows faced in red brick. With its refurbished garden it provides a welcome oasis in the centre of Hanwell. There are, at the time of writing, two Sunday services and the church is also open for prayer three days in the week. Note the unadorned road in the old picture compared to the modern picture, which shows extensive markings.

UNION CHURCH, WESTMINSTER ROAD, HANWELL

THE UNION CHURCH opened in 1901 with a congregation of 242. The gentleman in the inset is the Revd Allon Poole, who was minister from 1906 to 1914, having previously worked in New Zealand and other parts of London. Shortly after he began work in Hanwell, the reverend's eight-year-old son died. In 1959, the church merged with the Hanwell South Baptist Church, due to falling numbers. By the 1960s, the Scientology Church of Ealing used

the building and continued to do so until at least the 1970s.
It is now the Apostolic Catholic Assyrian Church of the East.
Unfortunately, the main part of the church has now been
knocked down; there is only a small part of the original
church still remaining.

Rev Allon Poole.

CHURCH OF OUR LADY AND ST JOSEPH, HANWELL

THE FIRST CHURCH on this site was built in 1864, with Pugin as the architect. It was a low building with a wooden roof and wooden columns. There was also a convalescent home for poor Catholic women next door. A new church – St Joseph's – replaced this one a hundred years later,

being re-dedicated in 1967. The new church is strikingly modern in comparison, with a very unusual steeply pitched roof made of aluminium. It also has an interesting sculptured panel over the entrance doorway depicting the Holy Family, although the jagged roof of the new building has not found universal favour with architectural critics. There are now more services than ever; where there were two masses on a Sunday in 1914, now there are four, as well as other services throughout the week, including two on Saturdays. Now, as then, there are two confessions on a Sunday. Note the more rural aspect, as suggested by the shrubbery and trees in the older picture, all long gone.

MIDDLESEX
ASYLUM CHAPEL

THE ASYLUM CHAPEL
was built by the asylum's
resident engineer, Henry
Martin, in 1870. It took
just eleven months to
complete and was dedicated
on 11 November 1870
by Bishop Claughton,
Archdeacon of London
and Chaplain General
of the Armed Forces.
It was re-dedicated in
1960 by the Bishop of
London. North House is
to the left of the chapel,
which was originally the
first superintendent's
residence on the female
side. Originally it was called

West House, but when East House was knocked down it then was confusingly renamed North House. It is now used to train junior doctors. Unfortunately, a new curving retaining wall has been built just behind the chapel, so it is now difficult when photographing the chapel to get all of it in. Trees have grown up and now obscure much of North House. The chapel also housed the hospital museum from 1992 until 2005, when the collection was sent elsewhere. The chapel is still used for services. As with many of these pictures, the ubiquitous motorcar appears in the modern view.

LYCH GATE, PERIVALE

PERIVALE WAS EXTREMELY rural, comprising of fields and farms right up to the 1920s, and this picture offers a glimpse of this vanished world, especially on the right-hand side of the footpath. The building to the left of the postcard is the rectory, parts of which date from the fifteenth century. Unfortunately, despite a campaign to save it, the building was demolished in 1958 as repairs were prohibitively expensive. The lych gate may seem ancient, but was in fact quite modern, being erected in 1905 to the memory of Mrs Emma Boosey, a parishioner, though in 1960 there was the possibility of its demolition due to damage by vandals, but the feature remains. Even in the modern view you can still detect that Perivale has retained some of its rural identity. The church has been redundant since the 1970s, but from 1981 has been run as an arts centre by the Friends of St Mary's Perivale. Note the different notices on the right of each picture, the first prohibiting trespassers, the second only allowing cyclists and pedestrians on the footpath.

HOLY TRINITY CHURCH AND VICARAGE, SOUTHALL

HOLY TRINITY CHURCH was built in 1890 and consecrated in 1891. The builder was J. Dorey of Brentford, who, incidentally, also built St Mellitus Church in Hanwell. The church architect was J.W.T. Lee, the land being given by the

Earl of Jersey. The church is in the early English style of Kentish rag stone with Bath stone dressings. It has stained-glass windows, but unfortunately some of these were destroyed during the Second World War. The vicarage is now a hostel called Asha, but the building is still recognisable. In 1914, there were three services on Sundays, yet at the time of writing there is but one. The church's claim to historical fame is that on 8 August 1953, the grandfather of a future princess was married here. This was Ronald Goldsmith, who wed Dorothy Harrison; in 2011 their granddaughter, Kate Middleton, became Her Royal Highness Princess Catherine, Duchess of Cambridge.

ACTON PARK

THE EARLIER PICTURE shows Acton Park – the first park to be built in Acton, in 1888 – in all its Edwardian glory. No park would be without its central bandstand for local and visiting bands to play on summer days and on special occasions, and parks were often used for local celebrations of national events, including the Coronation of George V in 1911. There had been an earlier bandstand, but it fell into disrepair and so was rebuilt for the Coronation. Ironically, the park only

came into existence following much acrimonious debate centred around the cost involved, whether a park was necessary, and whether its chief purpose was in fact to enhance the value of neighbouring houses (owned by councillors). The park is still much in use for its original purpose, and the annual Acton Carnival is held here, but as the modern picture shows, its centre is no longer adorned by the bandstand. This fell into disrepair in 1938 and, in 1941, the council noted that it was in a 'dilapidated and dangerous state' and so ordered the borough engineers department to demolish it. Sadly, it was never replaced and as we can see a flowerbed now adorns the centre of the park.

DEAN PARK, WEST EALING

HERE WE SEE another set of contrasting views of Dean Park. In 1911, parks in Ealing were not designed for children's play, although many youngsters used them as such, except on Sundays when this was banned (until 1940). Instead we see formal flower gardens. We can also see some of the shops on Uxbridge

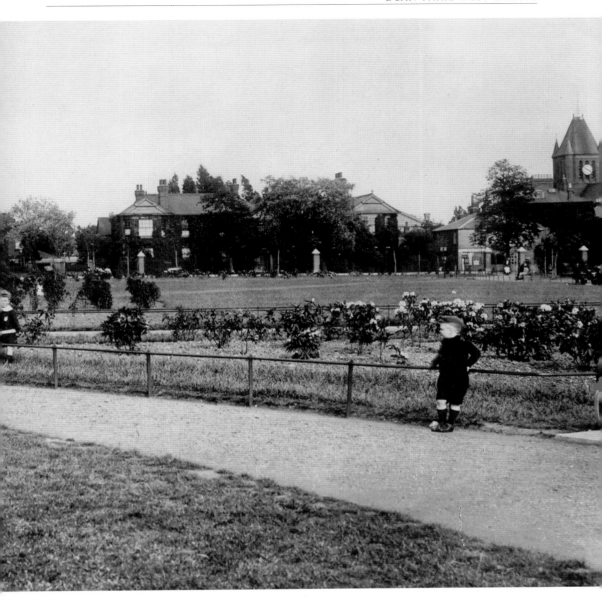

Road to the left. The buildings in the background, facing the east side of the park, are a mix. They are mostly domestic, but the one on the left is Ealing's Cottage Hospital, before it was transferred just before the First World War to Mattock Lane. On the far right is the tower of St John's Church. This part of the modern picture is now completely different, dominated as it is by the block of low-rise flats. The church tower can still be seen, but it lacks the spire visible in the earlier view due to a fire at the church in 1920, which destroyed much of the original building. Originally, allotments were on this site, but new land was found for them on Northfields Avenue.

RUSTIC BRIDGE,
WALPOLE PARK

THIS SOANESQUE FEATURE of Walpole Park appears much the same in the early twenty-first century as it did in the early twentieth. The bridge itself preceded John Soane, who owned the house between 1801 and 1810 and who mostly rebuilt it, adding embellishments to the feature in the park in order to transform the plain structure into

something which suggested antiquity – carved heads were incorporated to suggest the Middle Ages, while the bridge was intended to recall a Roman temple, with water flowing from it. There are a few changes, however. There is water in the pond, part of which can be seen in the foreground. In the 1920s, ornamental trees and shrubs were planted around the pond's sides. The public toilet in the background dates from about 1950, but may well be swept away as part of future plans to have the park and grounds refurbished, so that it more resembles the place during Soane's time, with a vista of the bridge along a larger and more open expanse. The bridge is today grade 2 listed.

HAVEN GREEN, EALING

THE VIEW ACROSS Haven Green towards the Parade is obscured by the trees in the modern picture, but, had it not been, the views would be far similar to that of the old image. However, the spire of Christ Church can be seen in both pictures. The buses in the modern view are evidence of the greater volume of traffic today, otherwise, there has been minimal change.

The border fence, the seats and the grass of Haven Green still exist. Haven Green itself dates back to at least the eighteenth century, as noted on maps of the time, but is probably older still. Originally it was much larger, extending southwards to the Uxbridge Road and also the north-east in 1741, when it was called Ealing's Haven. In 1777, it was called The Haven. However, despite its shrinkage, worse could have happened in 1945, when there were plans for a paddling pool, a fountain, toilets and a car park. Mr M.E.R. Jones, longstanding resident, protested that 'the adoption of any of these would at once destroy the amenities of this delightful part of the town'. It consists of 7 acres and was taken into the council's care in the 1870s.

LAMMAS PARK

EALING'S FIRST PARK, opened on 1 August 1883, on Lammas Day. The park was composed of 29 acres and cost £220 each. Charles Jones wrote of it, 'It was meant to contribute to Ealing's healthy nature'. In 1911 there were many facilities for leisure, including nineteen tennis courts, four croquet lawns, two bowling greens and three cricket pitches. There

was a Lammas Bowling Club and, in more recent times, a croquet club. This, until 1940, was the Ealing Park where games were played, unlike Walpole Park, which was designed as a haven for serenity and peace. However, until the 1890s, when the council purchased the remaining Lammas rights, cattle could still be grazed here and shortly after the park opened, a Mr Godfrey of Ranelagh Road was taking a stroll here when he was gored by a cow. Because it is further from Ealing's centre than Walpole Park, it attracts fewer visitors and events than its better-known neighbour.

37

CHURCHFIELDS RECREATION GROUND, HANWELL

CHURCHFIELDS RECREATION GROUND was Hanwell's first public park, opened in 1898. In the background is St Mary's Church, designed by Sir Gilbert Scott in 1841 and the third church to be built on the site. A hostile critic once wrote, 'The church itself is a poor thing, a sort of inferior brother to Turnham Green church; itself no delight, and designed in 1841 by the same, inevitable, Gilbert Scott, whose hand you find, unfortunately, everywhere'. The church is famous for the tomb of Jonas Hanway, the first man to use an umbrella in this country. Another interesting point is that Thomas Gainsborough's daughters are buried in the churchyard. Harry Secombe's brother, Fred, was at one time the rector of St Mary's. The view is much the same in both pictures.

CONOLLY DELL, HANWELL

CONOLLY DELL WAS originally part of the grounds of Lawn House (demolished in 1902) where Dr John Conolly, the third superintendent of the Middlesex County Asylum, resided. Conolly pioneered the system of non-restraint at the asylum and will always be remembered

for his work in this field. He resided at Lawn House from 1844 until his death in 1866, and ran a private asylum for young ladies at this establishment. The Dell (as it was known) was opened in 1912 and is Hanwell's smallest park, at just under 2 acres. The postcard shows the Conolly memorial to the left of the central flowerbed, erected in 1911. Originally it had a metal phoenix (the insignia of Hanwell Council from the 1890s onwards) on top of the memorial, but this is currently awaiting restoration. The memorial is now in a rather battered state and the beautifully kept flowerbed has also sadly vanished.

THE POND,
NORWOOD GREEN

THIS OLD CARD depicts children paddling in the Dutch canal on Norwood Green, an open space of about 10 acres. A children's play area now stands partially on the former site, although the modern photograph was taken just beyond this. The pond was filled in

because, in 1928, the council wanted to expand the adjacent Norwood Road. Furthermore, the pond had dried up and was being used as an unsightly rubbish dump. The elm trees, too, have gone, for in 1974 Dutch elm disease was spotted and, by 1977, all had been chopped down. The green is still used for sports.

PENSIONS OFFICE, ACTON

THIS IMPOSING BUILDING, on the east side of Bromyard Avenue, just north of the Uxbridge Road, is the headquarters of the Ministry of Pensions, and was erected for the accommodation of the large number of staff necessary to carry out the work in connection to the administration of about 3,000,000 war pensions. In the 1930s it was described thus: 'This building, which illustrates well the modern tendency in large scale architecture and has a real dignity in spite of its severe squareness of shape, is said to be the largest building under a single roof in the world'. In comparison, the more recent picture shows a less stark structure today, partly obscured by the many trees in front of it. The building is no longer home to civil servants but has been modernised and sold as private flats. In 2011, a one bedroom flat here – advertised as 'West London Apartments' – sold for £310,000. Another change can be seen in the windows, which have fewer glazed frames across them in the modern view.

HABERDASHERS' ASKE'S SCHOOL, ACTON

OPENED AS A livery school for girls in 1901, this was once one of the district's best public schools. This grand building, with a playground of 2 acres, and marked for tennis and hockey, cost £60,000. Looking at the two pictures, one could be excused for thinking that very little

had changed, save for the inevitable automobiles, the road markings, the lamp post and the iron gating. Yet this would be a mistake. Although the main structure still stands, this no longer Haberdashers' Aske's School, which moved to Elstree, Hertfordshire, in 1971, in order to be next to the company's boys' school. Cardinal Newman School in Acton briefly used the premises, but in 1987 it began to be used for its present use, that of the Japanese School. It accepts pupils aged between 6 and 16, and teaches both boys and girls. Ealing has one of the highest number of Japanese residents in Ealing, which is almost certainly due to this school.

BERRYMEDE PRIORY

THIS FINE OLD Gothic mansion, built in about 1802, is seen in the earlier picture in all its glory, despite standing in fewer acres of parkland than it once did. It was briefly used by an ecclesiastical body, and by the time this picture was taken had become the Acton

Constitutional (Conservative) Club. Ealing MP Herbert Nield was no stranger to its interior. The contrast with the modern picture could not be more telling. The car park in the contemporary picture, which is just south of Acton Town Hall, is the site of the Priory, though this is unclear to the casual passer-by. The twentieth century was unkind to large buildings of this kind, and those in and around London, even if they escaped the Blitz, often fell to developers. The local Conservatives sold the building to Nevill's bakery in the 1930s, but by 1977 the bakery was no more and it fell derelict. Although enjoying listed status, it was allowed to fall into such disrepair that the council decided on demolition on safety grounds in 1984.

GOLDSMITHS' ALMSHOUSES

THESE ALMSHOUSES, BUILT in 1811 for £1,200 by Goldsmiths' livery company, who owned much land in East Acton, have not altered much over the last two centuries, except for the fact that the foliage to the fore has obscured the entrance in the modern view. They were built for six elderly men and women, all of whom were to be connected to the

Goldsmiths' company. The architect was Charles Beazley, and the building is of brick, and consists of two storeys. The site was chosen because it was of poor quality soil and would not have been very agriculturally productive. A chapel is also attached to the building. The inmates were given an annual pension and were looked after by a superintendent, a matron and a labourer, but in the nineteenth century most had their own servant or a relative to help them. The company still administers the charity, but the almshouses, which are grade 2 listed, are today looked after by the Peabody Trust. The chapel has since been converted for use as another room as part of a recent refurbishment.

SOUTH EALING CEMETERY

THESE TWO VIEWS of the entrance gate to the cemetery are almost identical, save for increased foliage in the modern view. The two wings of the entrance are in fact the two chapels for the cemetery; one for Anglicans and one for nonconformists. The bell and clock were added in 1877. They were the work of Messrs Gillett and Bland of Croydon, and 'The machinery will

be so adapted as to toll the funeral bell'. The installation took much time and the scaffolding was unsightly. Finally, when the work was accomplished, the local press were of the opinion that 'it will, doubtless, prove a welcome guest to so many who pass that way'. The cemetery came about because the parish churchyard was almost full. So, the Ealing and Brentford Burial Board was formed in 1858 and 8 acres of land, bought in 1860, was laid out in the following year. Among those buried here is Spencer Walpole MP, once owner of Pitshanger Manor, politician, and the nearest person nineteenth-century Ealing had to a squire.

CALVADOS

THIS HOUSE IS on the south-east side of Hanger Lane and was built in about 1897 for Major General Joseph Godby, one of the many retired soldiers in Ealing of the time. Godby had served in the army as an artillery officer from 1846, seeing active service in the Crimean War and rising through the ranks as the decades passed. There were no trees to obscure the house from the road then, and hedges provided a degree of privacy for residents in the gardens. We can see from the contemporary view that the house is, essentially, externally the same over a hundred years later, although the hedges have gone and trees now shield the house. General Godby is no more, needless to say, having died five years after the earlier picture was taken whilst on his way from Dorking to London. The house changed its name on his departure, with John Percy, the next owner, renaming it Hotspur Lodge. The house no longer has a name, simply the unromantic number 13, as has been the case since about 1914. Unlike most pictures in this book, this old view is a photograph rather than a postcard.

EALING TOWN HALL

THE TOWN HALL was designed by Charles Jones and opened by the Prince of Wales on 15 December 1888. In 1911, it was the centre of the borough's administration, housing all the council's officials as well as providing offices for the mayor and councillors, and a debating chamber. It is indeed an imposing building and has more than once being mistaken for a church. By 2011, there have been many changes, not all of which are apparent from

EALING
TOWN HALL.

RESPICE · PROSPICE

EALING.

these two pictures. Firstly, the building was extended to the east in 1930, and an annexe was built behind the Town Hall in the 1960s (though this was demolished in 2010 to make way for a new complex of shops and flats). Secondly, just to the left of this picture is the council's main administration unit, Perceval House, which houses most of the council's administrative staff. These changes came about because of the huge expansion of council employment in the past century. Yet much remains the same, with the council's debating chamber, mayoral offices and some administrative staff still being based in this building, which is somewhat overshadowed in size, if not in elegance, by the aforementioned Perceval House.

ST ANN'S SCHOOL, HANWELL

ST ANN'S SCHOOL was built in 1902 in Springfield Road, Hanwell, by the School Board, initially as an elementary school for infants and juniors aged from five to twelve years. There was once a village well that has now been covered over in the playground of the school, although no evidence of this can be seen today. The school is located in a quiet suburban backwater and the building has retained its original features to this day. The old postcard shows snow on the playground and a low wooden fence that would now

be impractical. The modern view shows a very prominent blue metal fence that rather spoils the appearance of the school, but is a safety feature. In the intervening years, the school became a Secondary Modern School for Girls, then a mixed middle school by the 1960s, and, since 1982, has been a school for disabled children aged between 11 and 19.

MANOR HOUSE, SOUTHALL

THIS HEAVILY RESTORED and much altered manor house in Southall dates from the sixteenth century and formerly belonged to the Awsiter family. The manor house was also once owned by William Thomas, an inventor of a unique type of sewing machine in the late nineteenth century. The manor house was bought by the Council in 1913 to use as offices, and is today used by the local Chamber of Commerce. The contemporary picture shows

the manor house undergoing much needed and long-overdue restoration, with scaffolding up all around the building and looking cluttered and undignified. It is hoped that once the work has been completed the manor house will once again reveal itself as a unique building of great character and charm.

OTTO MONSTED'S
MARGARINE FACTORY,
SOUTHALL

THIS POSTCARD SHOWS what good transport links the margarine factory had in Southall. A branch railway links to the GWR network on the left of the card, taking goods trains to the Brentford Docks on the River Thames. The factory was also situated not far from the

Grand Union Canal, formally the Grand Junction Canal. Otto Monsted was of Danish origin and originally set up his factory in Godley in Cheshire, but moved to Southall because of the better transport links to central London. At the time, it was the biggest margarine factory in Europe, opening in 1895, and existed until 1929. It closed because the move to pre-packaging would have been too expensive and there was no room for expansion. The building still standing was the Maypole, which was used by the employees as a clubhouse and had a billiards room and a library. It dates from 1910 and cost £15,000. More recently, it was in use as the Southall Community Centre, but at the time of writing its future is uncertain.

TWYFORD AVENUE

THIS TREE-LINED street has seen several changes over the years yet has retained some of its character. It is hard not to be struck by the earlier picture's broad, empty street and equally spacious pavements. The modern picture is cluttered by parked vehicles and cars travelling down the road. The speed bumps in the modern view are a mute witness to the need to curb their speed, and the bollards to the left are a deterrent against cars parking on

the pavement. Yet we must allow the more recent improvements of the streetlights. William King-Baker, an Acton resident, wrote in 1912 that the road was 'where some members of the district council reside – a wide shady avenue more readily corresponding to the open attractiveness of a modern Canadian city, like Toronto, than any avenue of our town'. Over the years it has been called Mill Lane, New Road, Green Lane, and Wegg Avenue, before being settled on its current name in about 1901. During the Blitz, a house belonging to a Jewish family was hit and six people were killed. Another former inhabitant, who had a blue plaque erected to his memory in 2011, was Professor Titmuss, an academic who played a significant part in shaping social policy after the Second World War.

SPRINGFIELD PARK

SPRINGFIELD PARK IS neither a street name nor a house name, but a name given to a district in Acton just to the west of Horn Lane and close to a small open space called Springfield Park.

This house – known as Peacehaven – is at the eastern extreme of Cresswick Road, a fairly well-to-do district of Acton. Very little has changed of the external features of this house, which once housed residential accommodation of the International Friendship League. The few changes visible are fewer trees in the modern view and the hedge in the earlier view has been replace with a higher wall.

EAST ACTON LANE

INITIALLY THIS VIEW was part of the detached hamlet of East Acton, which existed of little more than a rural lane with housing on either side. The lane stretched northwards from the junction with Uxbridge Road, and the view here shows it at its northern end, with a junction eastwards to East Acton Green. Both views show the village green in the centre with the pub, The Goldsmith's Arms, behind it. The Green is now regulated under the Commons Registration Act.

EALING BROADWAY

THEN AS NOW, Ealing Broadway is the area's principal shopping street. However, the shops which compose it have altered considerably. Take the left-hand part of the views first; in the older view we have the domed shop of Eldred Sayers & Son, one of the two principal department stores of early twentieth-century Ealing. However, the modern view shows a different building, which is part of the Arcadia shopping centre. The shop occupying that

part of it was, until 2010, a branch of the music store HMV. The other prominent building on the left-hand side of the street was the Lyric Theatre, which has since been demolished. A branch of W.H. Smith's now stands on the site. On the other side of the road is John Sander's furniture store, the other premier store in Ealing a century ago. It has since been replaced by a branch of Marks & Spencers. Most of the other shops on the right of the older picture have been replaced by the Ealing Broadway shopping centre. In the background of each picture is a bank. Although the bank is today a branch of NatWest, the building itself remains unaltered. Unlike the earlier picture, from around 1911, standing in the middle of the road today is not advised.

CASTLE HILL AND
DRAYTON COURT, EALING

THE POSTCARD SHOWS the imposing Drayton Court, with a horse-drawn taxi rank outside and hut. The postcard is dated 1904, when the hotel was just six years old. It had twenty-five rooms, offered evening meals at two shillings each, had a billiards room for indoor recreation, and tennis courts and bowling greens outside. Guests could use it as a base for exploring the countryside that was Greenford and Perivale prior to 1920. This was before Ho Chi Minh worked as a waiter at Drayton Court around February 1914. At that time he went under the name of Nguyen Tat Thanh. There was a tale that Uncle Ho put a heated brick under his bed to keep warm during the long winter nights at the Drayton Court Hotel. Unfortunately, the trees now rather obscure the view of the hotel in the modern photograph, so it does not have quite the same atmosphere as the charming Edwardian postcard. Although the hotel ceased being residential in the 1960s, it has now been refurbished and offers rooms as well as a health suite. Note the different forms of transport: horse-drawn cabs in 1904, the less environmentally friendly motorcars in 2011.

MATTOCK LANE,
WALPOLE PARK, EALING

THIS ANCIENT THOROUGHFARE, dating from at least the eighteenth century, borders on the north side of what is now Walpole Park, and has a number of detached villas to its north. It is once known as Mattock Lane. The change shown in the contemporary picture was a result of decisions taken in the 1950s. After petrol rationing was over, increased car usage became universal in Britain, and Ealing was no exception. The council were concerned that there was

insufficient car parking
in central Ealing and so
proposed creating a car
park on the south side of
Mattock Lane. Mr M.E.R.
Jones wrote to complain,
'Mattock Lane, regarded
as the last of rural Ealing
in the centre of town,
has been turned into a
car park for the benefit of
the wretched motorist,
thus destroying forever its
peaceful country aspect'.
He claimed it would only
be used on Saturday
afternoons and by people
going to Questor's Theatre.
Another man wrote that
'ultra-modernising our
beauty spots is tragic'. Yet
in 1959, the council spent
£3,500 creating a space for
eighty-six cars to park.

PERIVALE

A REMARKABLY RURAL scene taken from the Argyll Road looking towards Horsenden Hill, with Perivale Lane off to the right. Notice the cart under the shade of the tree. At this time, the following description was given of Perivale: 'one can be in the sweetest, most rural, old world hamlet imaginable, within half a mile's walk from the centre of town [Ealing]'. Sadly, the modern scene is almost unrecognisable when compared to the original postcard. It is now an extremely busy road,

highlighting just how much Ealing has been swallowed up in the urban sprawl. This occurred largely in the 1930s, when industry and housing emerged in the aftermath of the building of Western Avenue.

SOUTHALL GREEN

THIS POSTCARD SHOWS two interesting
buildings along Norwood Road in the
Southall Green area. The Metropolitan
Bank on the corner of Adelaide Road is
still a bank, now the HSBC, but the White
Swan Hotel is now the Sri Guru Amardass
Gurdwara. It hosts smaller religious
ceremonies, with larger ones being held
at the vast temple on Havelock Road. In
1916, the landlord of the White Swan
Hotel was Alfred Standley. The hotel began
life in about 1860, but closed in the 1990s.
The Metropolitan Bank was founded in
Birmingham in 1829. It merged with the
London, City and Midland Bank in 1914,
which became simply the Midland Bank in
1924, then the HSBC in 2001. The London

City and Midland Bank also had branches in Acton, Chiswick, Ealing and Ealing Common, and doubtless many more, with its head office in Threadneedle Street. The date on Adelaide Road side of the building says 1903. Another view which is, remarkably, little changed.

THE PARADE

VARIOUS FORMS OF transport dominate these views. Note the horse-drawn cab rank, full of cabs ready to take passengers, and the hut on the left for the men to take a break. With commuters leaving the railway stations and desiring a quick trip home, the cab rank was ideally placed. The same can be said of the taxi-cabs in 2011, except these cabs are powered by the internal combustion engine. Also, note the prominent District line underground station on the right of the old picture, with its adverts prominently displayed. The same building exists today, but since the 1960s no longer houses a railway station (it has merged with the GWR station and is situated just out of frame to the right), but a number of shops. Other changes are the elimination of the Tudoresque building on the right, and the erection of the tower block in the background of the contemporary photograph. We have also lost some of the trees in the background, but the shops to the left of the District line station still exist.

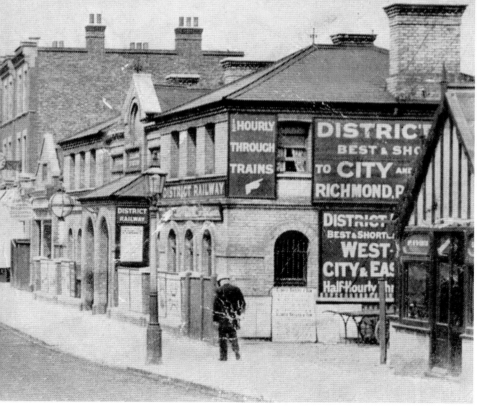

LOWER BOSTON
MANOR ROAD, HANWELL

THIS POSTCARD DEPICTS the number 13 tram, complete with driver and conductor. This tramway connected the Bath Road, near Brentford, and the Uxbridge Road, just over two miles to the north. It was built by the London United Electric Tramway Company between May 1905 and June 1906, and initially the charge was a penny in either direction. Notice

the Home and Colonial store on the left-hand side of picture. Also note that the modern E8 bus has the same destination – Brentford – as the number 13 tram, even though separated by all those years! The trams were withdrawn in December 1936 and were replaced by trolleybuses, themselves replaced by buses in 1962. The trams, incidentally, became single-deckers in 1924. Notice the man holding a pram in the postcard.

BRENT BRIDGE, HANWELL

THIS IS AN interesting postcard, as it shows part of the grounds of the County of Middlesex Asylum on the left-hand side. Note how the trees have been planted along the perimeter of the wall to screen off the view of the asylum from the general public. There is only one small section of this wall still intact today and the area is now completely open – the former asylum grounds now form part of the car park for Ealing Hospital. The first stop in the opposite

direction to which the tram is travelling was called 'The Asylum Gates'. The postcard is also interesting in its depiction of different forms of transport. Note the advertisement on the tram for Gossages military pickle.

Just as now, public transport served as an excellent medium for advertisements. Also, note the more built-up scene in the modern view in contrast to the earlier rural one.

TRAM CROSSING BRENT BRIDGE, HANWELL

THE OLD POSTCARD depicts a charmingly rural scene, apart from the tram crossing over the bridge that is. The bridge is perfectly framed by the tall trees growing on either side of the riverbanks. The tramway was part of that built from March 1901 until July of the same year

and was opened on the 10th. It was a five-mile track from Shepherd's Bush to Southall and was extended westwards to Uxbridge in 1904. Each tram could carry sixty-nine passengers and, on average, 50,000 people used the service each day. The contemporary photograph shows the new Brent Bridge. There is no longer access to the right-hand side bank, so the photograph had to be taken as near as possible to the postcard view, and a considerable time was needed to line-up a bus in exactly the right position. As with the Brentford – Hanwell route, trams were replaced by trolleybuses in 1936, and by buses in 1962.

RECREATION GROUND
AND WHARNCLIFFE
VIADUCT, HANWELL

THIS IS A lovely view of a lady brandishing her umbrella at a boy in this postcard. The bandstand was built in 1905, at a time when local bands, such as that of the branch of the Salvation Army and Hanwell's Silver Band, gave public performances on summer weekends (see also pages 28-29). It was removed in 1953 as it had fallen into disrepair. The view of the Wharncliffe Viaduct (one of Isambard Kingdom Brunel's first major works, built in 1836-1838), though, is still recognisable. This was Queen Victoria's favourite route from London to Windsor, and would have commanded fine views of the surrounding area from the viaduct. It took a considerable time to get a train in the modern photograph to line up roughly in the same position as in the postcard!

IRON BRIDGE, SOUTHALL

BRUNEL'S BRIDGE TOOK the Great Western Railway across the Uxbridge Road. The present bridge of wrought iron was constructed in 1847, as the first bridge collapsed several times. The old view is a promotional postcard for the AEC factory that was very close by and shows

the vehicles that the company produced. AEC built most of London's buses from the 1920s to the 1970s; many later ended up in Malta. The view is similar to that now, though AEC have long disappeared, folding in 1979. The advertising is still there, but in a different location and advertising different products.

THE 'THREE BRIDGES', SOUTHALL

THIS CARD SHOWS a unique crossing of three main features, the road, canal and railway, and is possibly the only place where all three intersect in the country. The road

bridge crosses the canal, which was channelled into a purpose-built iron trough and the railway goes underneath this. It is known as the Three Bridges, but only really has two bridges, as the railway runs on the ground. The canal was diverted through the grounds of the asylum while it was under construction. This was Isambard Kingdom Brunel's last major work, as he died shortly after completing this structure, which opened in 1859. Unfortunately, access to the railway embankment was impossible, so, unlike the photographer for the postcard, it was necessary to lean over the road bridge to take the modern view.

CANAL AND NORWOOD
BRIDGE, SOUTHALL

THE CHILDREN DEPICTED in this old view rather enliven this canal-side photograph. Today, only the slightly offset bridge leading to Adelaide Dock is recognisable. The cottage, which is just visible on the left, was one of six, and has now gone because they were no longer fit for human habitation. Norwood Bridge has been replaced and is set further back than the old bridge, so an identical photograph could not be taken. Adelaide Dock was built in the 1850s for the steam-powered Norwood Flour Mills, and was situated on the west side of Norwood Bridge.

If you enjoyed reading this book, then you may also like . . .

Paranormal London

NEIL ARNOLD

From sightings of big cats such as the Southwark Puma and the Cricklewood Lynx to the terrifying tales of the Highgate Vampire and Spring-Heeled Jack, along with stories of mermaids, dragons, fairies and alien encounters, this enthralling volume draws together a bizarre and intriguing collection of first-hand accounts and long-forgotten archive reports from the capital's history.

978 0 7524 5591 4

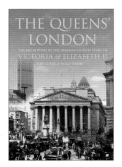

The Queens' London: The Metropolis in the Diamond Jubilee Years of Victoria & Elizabeth II

JON CURRY & HUGO SIMMS

In 1897, *The Queen's London* was produced to commemorate the Diamond Jubilee of her most excellent Majesty Victoria, Queen of Great Britain and Ireland and Empress of India. In 2012, *The Queens' London* pairs these beautiful vintage views with 180 images taken from identical vantage points in London, offering a fascinating perspective on the history behind London's familiar streets.

978 0 7524 7011 5

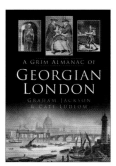

A Grim Almanac of Georgian London

GRAHAM JACKSON & CATE LUDLOW

From an anaconda attack at the Tower of London to a ghost in Regent's Park, a murder at the House of Commons, a body-snatching case, and a decapitated head in the churchyard of St Margaret's in Westminster, this book is sure to terrify, disgust and delight residents and visitors to the City alike. With 100 incredible illustrations from the rarest and most sensational true-crime publications of the age, no London bookshelf is complete without it!

978 0 7524 6170 0

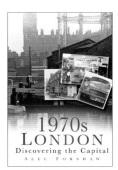

1970s London: Discovering the Capital

ALEC FORSHAW

London in the early 1970s was a city of declining industries and derelict docklands, a townscape blighted by undeveloped bomb sites and slum clearance schemes. It was a decade which saw the three-day week, the Notting Hill riots and the last of the anti-Vietnam war protests. This book portrays the London of over thirty years ago as it appeared to a young man in his twenties, stumbling across the sights and sounds of an extraordinary city

978 0 7524 5691 1.

Visit our website and discover thousands of other History Press books.

www.thehistorypress.co.uk